Ground cover plants

Cover illustration: *Geum borisii*

Overleaf: *Dicentra*, *Tiarella* and *Epimedium*.
Photographs by Michael Warren

Ground cover plants

A Wisley handbook

Cassell Ltd

The Royal Horticultural Society

Cassell Ltd.
1 Vincent Square
London, SW1P 2PN
for the Royal Horticultural Society

First published 1975
New edition, fully revised and reset 1985

British Library Cataloguing in Publication Data
Ground cover plants
1. Ground cover plants
I. Royal Horticultural Society
635.9'64 SB432

ISBN 0–304–31089–1

Photographs by Martyn Rix, Michael Warren
Design by Kwan Brenchley

Typeset by Georgia Origination Ltd., Formby
Printed and bound in Spain by Artes Graficás Grijelmo SA, Bilbao

Contents

Viola 'Huntercombe Purple', a plant which prefers a cool, open position. (see page 64)

Introduction

Ground cover is a term that has been often used in the horticultural literature of the last thirty years*. It is a technique of growing plants close together so that they make a continuous canopy of leaves over the soil. This canopy must be thick enough to prevent any other plants (i.e. weeds) from becoming established below it. The weeds will not thrive chiefly because of lack of light, but also because of root competition for water and nutrients. This situation is natural in the wild, where plants most suited to a particular environment will survive, flourish and smother the weaker plants. The difference in the garden is that the gardener, not the environment, chooses what is to grow and survive.

A garden is an artificial environment. Almost all our garden plants have either been introduced from other climates or bred for characters that would not necessarily allow them to survive in the wild in this country. All cultivation of garden plants is directed at creating and maintaining an artificial population. But in doing this it is sensible to adopt natural methods, as in the ground cover approach.

The theory of ground cover, therefore, is to use ornamental plants to cover areas of soil in the garden so thickly that no weeds can compete. In the modern interpretation the plants used must be those that can thrive with only minimum maintenance. Neither grass nor carpet bedding qualify, because although they fulfil the first requirement they need a lot of labour – grass must be regularly mowed to keep it looking controlled, and carpet bedding needs even more work in the annual production of new plants. The types of plant which do qualify are perennial and must be hardy for the area where they are to grow.

This gives a useful range of ornamental plants available in Britain. Many will be effective once established with the minimum of help from the gardener, and there are even more that can be used successfully with further encouragement for perhaps a rather longer period.

Although the technique is not really a new one, in its modern interpretation it is particularly advantageous in gardens with little available labour, and where there are fairly large areas which can sensibly and attractively be used for growing suitable ground-

*For a selection of books, see p.23.

cover plants. In general, appropriate plants to use will be of relatively low, spreading habit of growth; those with upright, open-branched growth are unsuitable as they allow plenty of light to reach the soil surface so that weeds will flourish. There is no clear dividing line between plants that are good as ground cover and those that are not, because in between the good and bad come many plants whose degree of success depends on the gardener and on the environment. Choosing suitable plants for the environment and encouraging them to grow well are the important factors for success with ground cover.

Some enthusiasts give the impression that almost all of the plant kingdom can be used as ground cover in one way or another. In practice this is not the case; only a proportion are satisfactory. When starting with ground cover in the garden, it is better to begin with easily controlled and easily cultivated plants. In this booklet is listed a selection of these (p.24). Few are ideal, because plants are always growing, and all have their disadvantages as well as advantages. Either they are easy to establish and will continue growing vigorously so that later they need to be restrained, or they need a good deal of attention to get them to flourish. Some start off well and are excellent for a year or two but then gradually deteriorate without attention. Guidance on advantages and disadvantages is given in the lists, but be prepared for some degree of compromise, depending on the situation and conditions of each individual garden.

Cytisus × *kewensis*, a hummock-forming plant with attractive lemon yellow flowers. (see page 33)

Why use ground cover?

The main reason for using the technique is to reduce the time spent on keeping the ground clear of weeds between the desirable plants. The effect of a complete carpet of plants gives an attractive natural appearance to the border.

Most people will still want some area of grass in the garden, for sitting out, and also because grass can be walked on without harm. No other ground cover has such tolerance to human traffic. But there are many other places where ground cover can be used instead of grass, for instance in shade, where grass will rarely grow well. Shade beneath trees is a special problem because the light conditions beneath a tree will change as the tree grows, and so after a few years the plants chosen initially for light shade may need to be replaced by other species that will tolerate a denser shade.

Grass banks are another problem garden feature, because, although they are easy to mow with the 'hovercraft' type of lawn mower, there is still an element of danger when mowing. An alternative is to plant permanent ground cover on the bank.

Shrub (including rose) borders too can be planted with lower ground cover plants so giving a pleasing community of varying heights. There is one problem that may arise with such a border and that is to keep the shrubs sufficiently well fed. With such a dense community of competing plants regular feeding is essential, usually with foliar nutrition (see p.23).

These are some special uses of ground cover plants, but a border in any part of the garden can be used, selecting the plants according to the aspect and soil. Often we achieve 'ground cover' without realising it, but to be effective it usually requires careful planning.

Above: Ground cover for a shady spot, *Ajuga*, ferns and feverfew.
Below: *Pernettya mucronata*, a coloniser which appreciates full sun and an acid soil. (see page 55)

Above: *Pulmonaria* 'Munstead Blue', an effective and tolerant plant. (see page 58)
Below: *Hypericum calycinum*, St John's wort, a rapidly growing dwarf shrub which will grow in any well drained soil. (see page 48)

What can be used?

Plants suitable for use as ground cover are nearly always perennials. Annuals and biennials are too short-lived to compete with weeds, although there may sometimes be a place for a spreading low-growing annual such as *Limnanthes douglasii* as a 'filler' in the first year between the permanent perennials.

Almost any plant which has a spreading habit of growth is in its way acting as ground cover. Although many species are recommended, it is as well to realise that a considerable number – hellebores, pulsatillas, *Claytonia sibirica* and various rock-plants like *Acantholimon* among them – which are suggested by some writers do not really fulfil the function of ground cover as defined here. This is usually because the foliage canopy they make is not dense enough to suppress the weeds effectively, or it is very slow to cover the ground.

The main requirements of a good ground cover plant are:–

(a) Hardiness, in an average winter, in the area concerned. As an example, *Hypericum calycinum* is usually hardy throughout Britain. *Osteospermum* (*Dimorphotheca*) 'Nairobi Purple', although an excellent ground cover, is less likely to survive the winter at Wisley than in Cornwall where winters are usually less severe.

(b) Tolerance of other adverse conditions, particularly periods of drought or extended wet weather.

(c) Sufficient vigour to cover the available ground in the first or second season after planting.

(d) The ability to form a dense, relatively low-growing cover and to remain in good condition for a number of years (at least 5 to 10) without requiring very much attention. Evergreens may be more effective in fulfilling this requirement, as deciduous plants, such as hostas, allow annual weed growth (chickweed, cleavers, and grass) to grow after the foliage has died down and particularly in early spring before their leaves have developed fully to cover the ground again.

(e) Maintain a degree of beauty and interest as garden plants during the year. Attractive flowers and/or fruits at some season or foliage interesting in shape, pattern, texture or colour are very desirable. Good foliage, particularly of evergreens, which will be seen by the gardener throughout the year, is most important. If not, one might just as well use ground elder!

(f) Low maintenance. An annual feeding or top-dressing and a clip-over or removal of dying foliage is all that should be needed. It should also be more or less free of the usual pests and diseases – spraying is work and costs money. Some evergreen ground-covers (and also deciduous plants like hostas) in damp conditions are havens for slugs and snails, which will require control.

There is therefore a wide range of plants, both woody and herbaceous, which fulful these requirements. But there are more factors to be considered in addition to the choice of plants – those of the particular garden conditions (soil, climate) in which the plants are to be grown. Here the gardener must make the best of the situation and the plants available.

Hosta ventricosa 'Variegata', one of a number of hostas with striking foliage. (see page 48)

Garden conditions

Every garden is different, in soil, in climate, and in the man-made environment of walls and wind funnels. These conditions can be altered to some extent, but a less laborious way of gardening is to choose plants that will grow well in the conditions existing, or with some relatively minor amendments to them.

First, these conditions must be analysed. In a small garden there will be quite a variation in the microclimate, even in the course of one day. One part has morning sun, one has evening sun, another has sun all day, or no sun at all. Combine these variations with those of rainfall, frost, wind during the year, and soil, and it is clear that plants have to be able to adapt to a range of varied conditions.

Rainfall cannot be controlled but can be supplemented if necessary by watering. The amount of sunshine in a particular position can be exploited by using plants that like the sun or those that grow best in the shade. Frost should only be a problem in exceptional years if hardy plants have been chosen.

Soils can be improved although it takes time. The ideal soil for most plants is a neutral loam, neither too light in texture (sand) nor too heavy (clay). There are few ideal soils, but much can be done to improve soil texture primarily by adding humus. Any type of humus can be used depending on what is available, garden compost, farmyard manure, leafmould, pulverised bark, mushroom compost (often alkaline), and peat are among suitable types most often available.

Less can be done to alter soil alkalinity or acidity, and it is a long-term process, so it is simpler to choose plants that are suited to the existing soil conditions. There are several soil testing kits on the market which will give an indication of the degree of soil acidity/alkalinity.

Light soils, derived from sands or chalk are easy to cultivate, even shortly after rain; they have good drainage, warm up quickly, but do not hold nutrients for long and dry out rather rapidly in summer. Heavy soils based on clays are sticky and should not be cultivated when wet (if soil structure is not to be damaged); they are slow to drain, warm up slowly in spring but hold nutrients well and maintain a good water supply in dry periods.

Types of ground cover plants

There are two main groups of herbaceous ground coverers – clump formers and colonisers. The first are relatively slow and steady growers, the second are fast growing but may in some instances produce a thinner canopy. Under 'herbaceous' are included bergenias and some epimediums, which keep their leaves over the winter, and so are not strictly herbaceous.

Shrubs too can be grouped in broadly the same way; those that produce a dense network of branches over several years, and those which spread more rapidly by rooting into the soil as they travel, or by producing suckers from underground roots. For gardeners ground cover plants have been grouped into several categories taking into account the type of cover they make. These divisions are arbitrary, and it is inevitable that there is some overlapping.

A. Quick growing evergreens with dense twiggy growth. These are the most efficient ground covers, and will make an almost complete canopy in the first year after planting at the distances recommended. Examples are certain cultivars of ivy (*Hedera helix*) and forms of the lesser periwinkle, *Vinca minor*.

B. Evergreens of dense growth which will take two seasons to cover the ground completely at the distances recommended. Alternatively, but more expensively, they can be planted closer together to obtain a good canopy in the first year. They may need extra encouragement, such as pruning, to stimulate more branching near the soil surface. *Erica carnea* (now *E. herbacea*), dwarf junipers and *Aurinia* (*Alyssum*) *saxatilis* are examples of these hummock forming or slow carpeters.

C. Deciduous clump-forming plants, which make thick cover with their leaves during the growing season, but die down during winter. Although there is no cover at that time their dense network of roots competes to some extent with annual weeds that may try to grow in the winter; but they are not completely effective ground covers and early spring weeding to remove weeds such as chickweed and annual meadow grass is often necessary. These are the slow but steady herbaceous type; examples are hemerocallis (daylilies), hostas, *Alchemilla mollis* and geraniums such as *G. wallichianum* which, although wide spreading, does not (or very rarely) root at the nodes.

D. Colonisers, deciduous or evergreen, which either make a

network of stems over the ground, rooting into the soil as they travel, or send out stolons or sucker growths, often from their roots. These often cover the soil area rapidly, but not all make such a dense cover as groups A to C, even in summer. Eventually they form thick mats of growth but during the first season before cover is complete they are likely to need regular weeding. Examples are *Duchesnea* (*Fragaria*) *indica*, *Glechoma hederacea* 'Variegata' and acaenas.

E. The last group of ground cover plants includes trailers which do not generally branch and root so much but have an 'umbrella-spoke' habit; they may be deciduous or evergreen. Because of their long growths these plants take longer than the earlier groups to make a thick cover and the gardener needs to have patience. Examples are some *Rubus* species, *Rosa* 'Max Graf' and *Clematis*. They have the considerable drawback of requiring at least two years of weed control and this is not always easy to carry out. In some situations, particularly on banks, they have their uses, but weed control is essential initially if they are to be successful.

There are two further groups to be mentioned, but with reservations.

F. The first is a group that is very successful, and often so vigorous that unless regularly restrained may swamp their neighbours. Such plants can sometimes be as much trouble as the following group, because of the amount of attention they need. Among them we include the various climbers sometimes suggested (e.g. the honeysuckles, *Lonicera japonica halliana* and *L. henryi*) which make a good canopy, but need considerable and regular control, unless they are planted in areas where they have room to spread without strangling their neighbours.

G. The other is of plants which are recommended by those whose enthusiasm for ground cover plants is all-embracing – who believe that any plant will serve. Many, however, are unsatisfactory, seldom if ever producing an efficient weed suppressing cover.

The aim of this book is to guide gardeners to plants that will be effective without constantly long-term attention and we believe that the lists on pp.26–64 contain a selection of the most satisfactory and reliable plants for the purpose.

Preparing to plant

To grow any plant successfully a favourable environment needs to be created and maintained. Almost all garden plants are incomers, expected to grow in an unaccustomed climate and to compete with the natives, which are well adapted to the environment. The chosen plants need all the help they can get from the gardener to become established and to compete successfully.

Having decided where the plants are to grow, the next requirements are to provide a soil bed in good condition for plant growth, and to remove all competitors, i.e. weeds. It is particularly important to eliminate perennial weeds before planting because afterwards it is almost impossible to get out the deep rooting and persistent weeds without uprooting the other plants.

CONTROL OF ANNUAL WEEDS

Annual weeds are a relatively straightforward problem as they are mostly shallow rooting and can be easily removed when forking over the soil before planting. With sensible precautions it is also possible to use certain herbicides to prevent the germination of weed seeds in the areas between the freshly planted ground cover and to eliminate seedlings of annual weeds.

Once ground cover plants are well established they should prove a cover sufficiently dense to inhibit or prevent germination of weed seeds, but weed control may be necessary in the first season or two after planting.

Commercially simazine and lenacil are used to control germinating weeds amongst many established, and newly planted, shrubby and herbaceous plants. Application is made to weed-free soil in early spring, the herbicides persisting for considerable periods. Susceptibility of cultivated plants varies considerably however, and quite a number of plants may suffer damage, risk of damage increasing on light sandy soils. At present there are no lenacil preparations marketed for use by the amateur for this purpose, but simazine is available.

CONTROL OF PERENNIAL WEEDS

It cannot be overemphasised that it is essential to remove all perennial weeds before planting any areas of ground cover.

Perennial weed species such as ground elder, couch grass and bindweed will compete with ground cover and are almost impossible to control once ground cover has been planted.

Both mechanical and chemical methods can be used to remove them. Allow a reasonable interval between treatment and planting so that if the weeds have not been completely eliminated there is an opportunity to see and treat any regrowth. By mechanical methods is meant weed removal by hand, by hoe, spade or machine. The last is only feasible before planting; the second and third are not recommended after planting, and the first can be done at any time. The choice between mechanical or chemical methods for control is not always straightforward. Mechanical removal of weeds can be carried out at any time of the year, but control by some chemical herbicides needs careful timing to achieve best results. Chemical herbicides must always be used very carefully, and are safest when used on unplanted ground. When garden plants are in the ground in which weeds are to be controlled it is frequently better to remove weeds by digging or hoeing rather than to attempt to use chemicals.

It is not possible in this booklet to provide detailed recommendations for the control of perennial weeds before planting. Much depends on local conditions e.g. soil type, although advice on weed control is available through the Society's advisory service.

Where the ground is infested with such persistent weeds as ground elder or horsetail, there should be no plans for planting until these pernicious weeds have been completely removed, by chemical and/or mechanical means.

PREPARATION OF THE SOIL

Many people believe that ground cover plants will grow without any particular care in soil preparation. This is a fallacy and may account for the poor results obtained with ground cover in some cases. It is most important to realise that for ground cover plants to grow well and remain in good condition for some years it is just as essential to prepare the soil properly as it is for roses.

However, a soil which is naturally fertile and of good structure is exceptional and most soils will benefit considerably from the incorporation of humus of some type by digging or rotovating it into the top soil layer.

Some different kinds of humus were listed on p.14. Whatever kind can be obtained it is dug in to a spade's depth, preferably in autumn, and the surface is left in a rough condition to weather over the winter. Humus incorporation and mechanical weed control can often be done in one operation.

Humus will improve most soil types, especially if applied regularly, increasing the water holding capacity of light soils, improving the drainage of heavier soils and providing some of the main nutrients for the plants. But nutrients are present in humus in only relatively small amounts (and hardly at all in most peats) and become available only slowly. An extra supply of nutrients in the soil will help plants to become established more quickly, and a general balanced fertilizer, such as Growmore, can be applied before planting, at a rate of 1 to 2 oz. per square yard (33 to 66g per sq. m.).

Ballota pseudodictamnus, a hummock-forming shrub grown for its fine grey foliage. (see page 29)

Planting

At one time the main planting season was during the autumn or early spring, because that was when plants were sent out from the nursery. Now that plants are available in containers at all seasons they can be planted at any time, but they must be cared for after planting, particularly in hot and dry weather, to make sure that they do not suffer from lack of water.

The best time for planting is still in late autumn or early spring, when the soil is starting to warm up and usually contains plenty of moisture, so that the roots are soon encouraged to grow.

The method is the same for all plants. Be sure that the hole is wide enough to take the roots without cramping them and deep enough to take the roots or the soil ball so that the newly planted plant is at the same level in the border as it was in the nursery or container. With container plants it is easy to be sure that they are neither too deep nor too high; the soil level in the container is the guide. With bare-root shrubs there will be a mark on the stem which shows the level that the soil in the nursery came to before lifting, so make sure that the soil after planting in the new position comes to the same level. With bare-root herbaceous plants, see that the collar of the plant, where roots and shoots join, is at soil level. When planting bare-root plants do not allow the roots to dry out while they are waiting to be put in – sun and spring winds can sometimes dry out fibrous roots very quickly, so cover the roots with some sheeting or sacking.

When the plant is in the right position, return the soil round the plant and firm it in well all round, finally forking over the surface to make it look tidy.

Spacing at the planting stage depends on the following factors:–

1. Type of ground cover (see p.15) i.e. how quickly the plants will cover a given area. (See also the recommended planting distances for individual species and cultivars in the tabulated list.)

2. Ultimate spread of the plants. This does depend to some extent on the environmental conditions, e.g. on the fertility of the soil.

3. Size of the plants at planting.

All of these factors need to be correlated to determine the spacing, for the sooner the neighbouring plants meet, the better for weed control. Smaller, younger plants tend to grow more

Liriope muscari, a clump forming plant with attractive purple flowers in autumn. (see page 51)

rapidly than larger, older plants because of their greater vigour. But the size of the plants and their cost does also have a bearing on the spacing and eventual coverage. Eight small plants spaced at 18 inches (45 cm) apart may cover the same area more efficiently in the first season than six large plants, planted at three feet apart.

However, when planting a larger area it may be too expensive to plant for the optimum effect as soon as possible, and so the plants are put in at wider spacing, with the commitment to continue weeding for two seasons instead of one.

Many, but not all, nursery catalogues give an idea of the spread of the plants, but if buying from a good garden centre there should be someone who can guide the buyer on this. A better idea is to see the plants growing in other people's gardens. There are also ground cover demonstration plots at the R.H.S. Garden at Wisley in Surrey, and at the Royal Botanic Garden in Edinburgh, where one can see the spacings used for the different types of plants, and their effect.

Maintenance

Once the plants are in, the weed control programme needs to be started and continued regularly, either by hoeing, by herbicides (see p.17), by interplanting (e.g. with annuals) or by mulching. In the first year after planting it is vital to give consistent weed control so that any competition for nutrients and water by other plants is kept to a minimum.

Hoeing or removal by hand of annual weeds as soon as they are seen is the most effective method. If this is done regularly as the seedlings germinate then there should be no problem.

Herbicides should always be used with care, and can only be suggested for emergency treatment when individual and persistent perennial weeds, such as dandelions and nettles, have escaped the initial clearance.

If available, a thick layer (two to three inches thick) of mulching material placed between the freshly planted ground cover is an excellent method of suppressing weed growth and it is beneficial in encouraging the rapid development of the plants. It is important to ensure that the mulch is not contaminated with weed seeds (often a problem with home-made compost) and to remember that many types of mulch are excellent seed beds for wind-blown seeds. But it may be a consolation that the seedlings that do germinate in a good mulch often grow so lushly that they are easy to pluck out. Peat and pulverized bark are two commonly available materials used for mulching.

It is important that the mulch goes between the plants and not on top of the growing shoots of the herbaceous plants which may be smothered themselves. Regular mulching in spring between the clump formers until they meet will help weed control and also feed the plants. Once they have spread into each other it is difficult to get the mulch beneath the plants and on to the soil. A thick layer of mulching material should not be put on top of colonisers because it would smother them, but a thinner layer sprinkled between the stems each year in spring will help to keep some humus supplied to the soil.

Fertilizers are not often applied to ground cover in gardens but they should be and will improve growth, and keep it vigorous. Early spring is the time to apply most fertilizers which may be one of the general artificial fertilizers (such as Growmore) or an organic fertilizer such as bone meal. Slow release fertilizers, e.g. Osmocote and Enmag, can also be very useful. They are more expensive than other fertilizers, but are formulated to release nutrients into the soil over a much longer period. Apply the fertilizer carefully to the soil around the plants in spring and not onto the foliage as some artificials may scorch the leaves.

Foliar feeding is sometimes recommended for plants. This is the application of a diluted liquid feed by spraying on to the leaves which quickly take in the nutrients. Foliar feeding will produce a rapid response from the plant, if applied at the right time, and quickly stimulates plant growth. The most effective times to apply foliar feeds are in late spring and early summer, when extension growth is normally being produced.

Its main value is to reinvigorate and feed plants that are backward in growth, such as those with a poor root system (perhaps due to drought) or one that is not yet established. It can also be useful as a quick feed for shrubs in a border thickly planted with ground cover (see p.9) but healthy well-grown plants should not normally need such a life-saving technique.

Pruning. Keeping the plants tidy is an occasional job which will be needed for certain plants – those that are very vigorous and need to be restrained from swamping other plants, and those that become straggly after several years and need to be cut back, such as ericas. The removal of dead twigs and old flowering stems is also part of regular pruning.

With some woody plants winter pruning may be necessary in the early years after planting to encourage branching near ground level.

FURTHER READING

Plants for Ground Cover by Graham Stuart Thomas (Dent) is the most comprehensive British book on the subject, but in *Ground Cover Plants* by Margery Fish (Collingridge) and *Foliage Plants* by Christopher Lloyd (Collins) there is also information on many suitable plants.

In addition there are many books on shrubs and herbaceous plants which include useful information on those suitable for ground cover. These include *Perennial Garden Plants* by Graham Stuart Thomas (Dent), Bean's *Trees and Shrubs Hardy in the British Isles*, eighth edition (John Murray), and *The Dictionary of Garden Plants in Colour* by Roy Hay and Patrick Synge (Michael Joseph).

List of plants

The following list contains information on plants suitable for ground cover. The additional notes on the column headings given below should be remembered when reading the tabulated lists.

Name of Plant. The species or hybrid group name is used for the main heading in most instances; appropriate clones are mentioned in the Special Remarks column to avoid repetition unless a particular clone is outstanding when it may be listed separately.

Group. The general habit and ground covering potential of Groups A–D are described on pp.15–16 but are repeated briefly here. They are given in the columns of the table of ground cover plants which follow.

Group A: Evergreen; Rapid growth; High density; Colonisers.
Group B: Evergreen; Medium to slow growth; High to medium density cover; Hummock forming or colonisers.
Group C: Deciduous; Medium to slow growth; High to medium density cover in summer; Clump forming, sometimes from winter rosettes.
Group D: Deciduous or Evergreen; Rapid to medium growth; High to medium density but usually requiring some weeding in first season (or two); Colonisers.

Colonisers. All those which normally produce roots from the stem 'joints' as they spread are tabulated as 'carpeters' whilst those which spread by means of underground shoots, suckers or stolons are tabulated as 'suckering'.

Hummock. Hummock formers usually have a central low stem with many wide-spreading branches. The stems occasionally root down and become 'Carpeting'.

Clump. Entirely deciduous plants growing in spring from winter buds or overwintered rosettes.

Plants from Groups E and F (see p.16) are with few exceptions omitted from the lists as they do not adequately fulfil the requirements for ground cover as defined in this booklet. Some plants in these groups can certainly be used successfully but are not described here; information on them is available from the references quoted in the bibliography.

Approximate height in inches and centimetres is given in column 5. This is the height of the plant when not in flower.

Planting distances. The figures, given in inches and centimetres refer to recommended distances for planting to obtain 75 to 100% cover within 12 to 24 months. The percentage coverage over this period may vary to a certain extent depending on climate, soil and other factors.

Special remarks. This column includes appropriate details of limitations of soil, climate and other factors; and details of cultivars recommended. No attempt is made to describe the plants fully as details are readily available in the references listed, and also in nursery catalogues.

Blechnum spicant, the hard fern, a lover of moist soils, and a plant with high tolerance of shade. (see page 29)

Name	*Group & Habit*	*Speed of Growth*	*Density of Cover*	*Approx. Height inches (cm)*	*Average Planting Distance inches (cm)*	*Shade Tolerance*	*Special Remarks*
Acaena novae-zelandiae	D Coloniser (Carpeter) d	Rapid	Medium	3–4 (8–10)	15–28 (38–70)	Low	Sun and well drained soil. Roots at nodes. *A. caesiglauca* and other species are also effective but the density of cover is variable.
Acanthus mollis var. *latifolius*	C Clump d	Medium	High	36 (90)	36 (90)	High	Handsome foliage and dense summer cover. Propagates itself by suckers.
Ajuga reptans (Bugle)	D Coloniser e	Medium	High	2–5 (5–13)	9–15 (23–38)	Medium	'Atropurpurea' and 'Rainbow' have attractive foliage colouring well in sun. 'Jungle Beauty' is a large, green leaved, vigorous cultivar. Needs moist soil and good conditions to avoid becoming bare in centre. Requires feeding.
Alchemilla mollis	C clump d	Medium	High	6–9 (15–23)	15–18 (38–46)	Medium	Attractive greeny-yellow flower sprays. Dense summer cover. Cut off flowers to prevent seeding. Division may be needed after about five years.
Antennaria dioica	D (Carpeter) e	Medium-slow	Medium	1–2 (2–5)	9 (23)	Low	Weeding required in first year.

Name	*Group & Habit*	*Speed of Growth*	*Density of Cover*	*Approx. Height inches (cm)*	*Average Planting Distance inches (cm)*	*Shade Tolerance*	*Special Remarks*
Anthemis cupaniana	B Hummock e	Medium	High	9 (23)	18–24 (46–60)	Very low	Sun and well-drained soil. Grey foliage. May not grow well in wet climates and seasons.
Anthemis nobilis (Chamomile)	D Coloniser e	Medium	Medium	1–3 (2–8)	9–15 (23–38)	Low	'Treneague' is the best non-flowering clone. Apt to die out in patches. Replace with young plants when it does this.
Arabis caucasica	B Hummock e	Medium	High	5 (13)	9–15 (23–38)	Low	'Flore Pleno' with double flowers and 'Variegata' with cream edged foliage also form good ground cover. Apt to die back in centre in poorly drained soil and becomes straggly in shade.
Arctostaphylos uva-ursi	B e	Medium-slow	Medium	6 (15)	15 (38)	Medium	Acid soils only. Carpeter, rooting down into rich soil.
Artemisia canescens	D Coloniser (Suckers) e	Medium	Medium	9–12 (23–30)	15–18 (38–46)	Low	Grey filigree foliage. Full sun or growth is sparse.

Deciduous = d Evergreen = e Semi-evergreen = s-e

Name	*Group & Habit*	*Speed of Growth*	*Density of Cover*	*Approx. Height inches (cm)*	*Average Planting Distance inches (cm)*	*Shade Tolerance*	*Special Remarks*
Artemisia stelleriana (see p.35)	D Coloniser (Suckers) e	Medium	High	12 (30)	18–24 (46–60)	Low	Grey foliage. Full sun.
Arundinaria viridistriata	D Coloniser (Suckers) e	Medium	Medium	24 (60)	24 (60)	Medium	Golden variegated leaves. Sometimes less dense at the edges of the clumps.
Asarum europaeum	B Carpeter e	Medium-slow	High	3–4 (8–10)	9–12 (23–30)	High	Useful in shade. Not in very dry positions. Other species including *A. canadense* and *A. shuttleworthii* are less dense.
Asperula odorata (Sweet woodruff)	D Coloniser (Suckers) d	Rapid	High	4–5 (10–13)	24 (60)	High	Invasive but attractive. Dense summer cover.
Aubrieta deltoidea	B Hummock e	Medium	High	3–4 (7–10)	12 (30)	Low	Sunny position. When growth becomes straggly cut back after flowering to rejuvenate.

Name	*Group & Habit*	*Speed of Growth*	*Density of Cover*	*Approx. Height inches (cm)*	*Average Planting Distance inches (cm)*	*Shade Tolerance*	*Special Remarks*
Aurinia (*Alyssum*) *saxatilis*	B Hummock e	Medium	High	9 (23)	15 (38)	Low	Sun; in shade tends to straggle. Yellow flowers. 'Citrinum' is as good with paler flowers.
Ballota pseudodictamnus (see p.19)	B Hummock e	Medium	High	9 (23)	15 (38)	Low	Sun. Dry position. Old growth should be cut back to main rosette in spring.
Bergenia species & hybrids (see p.35)	B Carpeter e	Medium-slow	Medium	5–12 (13–30)	9–24 (23–60)	Medium	Avoid *B. ciliata* and *B. ciliata ligulata* as foliage is often winter-damaged. 'Ballawley' may also sometimes be wind/cold damaged. Less flower and more straggling growth in dense shade.
Blechnum spicant (Hard fern)	D (Suckers) e	Medium-slow	Medium	9–15 (23–38)	12 (30)	High	Moist soils. Good in leaf mould under trees and shrubs. (see p.25)
Brunnera macrophylla	C Clump d	Medium	High	12 (30)	15–18 (38–46)	High	Blue flowers. Best in shade, leaves may scorch in sun in dry soils. Dense summer cover.

Deciduous = d Evergreen = e Semi-evergreen = s-e

Name	*Group & Habit*	*Speed of Growth*	*Density of Cover*	*Approx. Height inches (cm)*	*Average Planting Distance inches (cm)*	*Shade Tolerance*	*Special Remarks*
Calluna vulgaris (Heather)	B Hummock e	Medium	High	6–18 (15–46)	9–18 (23–46)	Medium-low	Acid soils. Many cultivars are useful as ground cover in full sun or slight shade. Clip over in spring to maintain compact habit.
Campanula portenschlagiana	D Coloniser d	Medium	High	3–4 (8–10)	9–12 (23–30)	Medium	Prefers sun. Attractive blue-purple flowers.
Campanula poscharskyana	D Coloniser (Suckers) e	Medium-rapid	High	3–4 (8–10)	12–15 (30–38)	Medium	Prefers sun. Attractive starry lilac-blue flowers. Can be invasive. 'E.K. Toogood' is similar but less rampant.
Ceanothus thyrsiflorus repens	B Hummock e	Medium	High	36 + (90 +)	36–48 (90–120)	Low	Hardy at Wisley (30 years on rock garden without protection). Full sun. Good for banks. Acid/alkaline soils.
Centaurea 'John Coutts'	D Coloniser (Suckers) d	Medium	Medium	6 (15)	12–15 (30–38)	Low	Grey foliage and attractive pink flowers. Full sun.
Cerastium tomentosum	B Carpeter e	Medium	High	6 (15)	15 (38)	Low	Rampant when established and liable to smother delicate plants, but useful in dry situations. Needs full sun. Straggly in shade.

Name	*Group & Habit*	*Speed of Growth*	*Density of Cover*	*Approx. Height inches (cm)*	*Average Planting Distance inches (cm)*	*Shade Tolerance*	*Special Remarks*
Ceratostigma plumbaginoides	D Coloniser (Suckers) d	Medium	Medium	9 (23)	12–15 (30–38)	Low	Sun. Blue flowers in late summer; attractive autumn foliage.
Cistus parviflorus (Rock rose)	B Hummock e	Medium	High	18–24 (46–60)	24–30 (60–75)	Low	Hardy at Wisley for over 20 years. Full sun: *C. salviifolius* 'Prostratus' and *C. lusitanicus decumbens* are good ground covers but less hardy.
Clematis orientalis	E Sprawling d	Rapid	High	24 (60)	72 (180)	Medium	Good for banks forming a tangled mass of growth. Yellow flowers.
Convolvulus cneorum	B Hummock e	Medium-slow	High	18–24 (46–60)	24 (60)	Low	Full sun. Good drainage. Not effective in cold gardens.
Cornus canadensis	D Coloniser (Suckers) d	Medium	Medium	4–6 (10–15)	12–15 (30–38)	Medium	Acid, fairly moist soils. Not in sandy dry soils.

Deciduous = d Evergreen = e Semi-evergreen = s-e

Name	*Group & Habit*	*Speed of Growth*	*Density of Cover*	*Approx. Height inches (cm)*	*Average Planting Distance inches (cm)*	*Shade Tolerance*	*Special Remarks*
Cotoneaster congestus	B Carpeter e	Medium-slow	High	3–4 (8–10)	12 (30)	Medium	Dense but relatively slow growth.
Cotoneaster conspicuus	B Hummock e	Medium	High	72 + (180 +)	60–72 (150–180)	Medium	'Decorus' is spreading in growth and forms large dense hummocks. Excellent for banks.
Cotoneaster dammeri	D Coloniser (Carpeter) e	Medium	Medium	3–4 (8–10)	24 (60)	Medium	Spreading thin growth at first; later dense, but hand weeding needed for the first year or two.
Cotoneaster 'Gnome'	B Carpeter e	Rapid	High	3–4 (8–10)	18–24 (46–60)	Medium	The best of several named prostrate cotoneasters for ground cover. Dense cover and neat foliage.
Cotoneaster microphyllus	B Hummock or Carpeter e	Medium-rapid	High	12–18 (30–46)	36–48 (90–120)	Medium	Dense growth, shoots rooting at the edges of the hammock. Var. *cochleatus* is shorter and as good.

Name	*Group & Habit*	*Speed of Growth*	*Density of Cover*	*Approx. Height inches (cm)*	*Average Planting Distance inches (cm)*	*Shade Tolerance*	*Special Remarks*
Cotula squalida	D Coloniser (Carpeter) e	Medium	Medium	1 (2)	9 (23)	Medium	Tolerant of dry or damp soils. Fairly invasive but good cover for dwarf bulbs.
Cytisus × kewensis (see p.8)	B Hummock d	Medium	Medium	12 (30)	24 (60)	Low	Full sun. Attractive primrose-yellow flowers.
Cytisus scoparius ssp. *maritimus*	B Hummock d	Medium-rapid	Medium-high	12–15 (30–38)	36 (90)	Low	Full sun. Hand-weeding is necessary in the first year.
Daboecia cantabrica (Irish heath)	B Hummock e	Medium	High	15–18 (38–46)	15–18 (38–46)	Low	Flowers purple to white. Acid soils only. 'Atropurpurea' is a vigorous deep-coloured clone. Forms of *D. azorica* are less reliable.
Dianthus (Garden pinks)	B Hummock e	Medium	High	9 (23)	9–12 (23–30)	Low	Full sun, alkaline soil. Many cultivars, e.g. 'Mrs Sinkins', 'Dad's Favourite' are suitable. (see p.35)

Deciduous = d Evergreen = e Semi-evergreen = s-e

Top: *Aubrieta* and *Arabis* tumbling over a rocky bank; both these plants are sun lovers. (see pages 27 & 28)
Above: A *Cotoneaster salicifolia* hybrid which produces striking berries

Above, left: Many Bergenias produce striking flower spikes (see page 29)
Above, right: *Artemisia stelleriana*, a sun-loving shrub grown for its feathery grey foliage. (see page 28)
Below, left: Forms of *Erica herbacea* (also known as *E. carnea*), the winter-flowering heath. (see page 37)
Below, right: *Dianthus* 'Dad's Favourite', a garden pink which prefers full sun and an alkaline soil. (see page 33)

Name	*Group & Habit*	*Speed of Growth*	*Density of Cover*	*Approx. Height inches (cm)*	*Average Planting Distance inches (cm)*	*Shade Tolerance*	*Special Remarks*
Dicentra formosa (see p.42)	D Coloniser (Suckers) d	Medium	Medium	9 (23)	15 (38)	High	Shade and moist soil.
Dryas octopetala (see p.42)	B Coloniser (Carpeter) e	Medium-slow	High	2–3 (5–8)	12–15 (30–38)	Low	Slow growing initially, eventually forming a dense mat. Full sun. Attractive white flowers and fluffy seed heads.
Duchesnea (Fragaria) indica	D Coloniser (Carpeter) e	Rapid	Medium	3 (8)	15 (38)	High	Strawberry-like foliage, yellow flowers. Vigorous and can be invasive. Only for rougher positions.
Epimedium perralderianum	D Coloniser (Suckers) e	Medium-slow	High	12 (30)	12 (30)	High	Excellent in shade or sun but of relatively slow growth. Yellow flowers. In 'leafy' soil. *E. pinnatum colchicum* and *E.* × *perralchicum* are equally good.
Epimedium × *versicolor*	D Coloniser (Suckers) d	Medium-slow	High	9 (23)	9 (23)	High	As *E. perralderianum* but deciduous and with pink and yellow flowers. Several clones, all good. *E.* × *rubrum* is of similar value. Cut off old leaf stalks in spring.

Name	*Group & Habit*	*Speed of Growth*	*Density of Cover*	*Approx. Height inches (cm)*	*Average Planting Distance inches (cm)*	*Shade Tolerance*	*Special Remarks*
Erica herbacea (*E. carnea*) (Winter-flowering heath)	B Hummock or Carpeter e	Medium	High	9 (23)	15 (38)	Medium	Best in open positions on acid (or slightly alkaline soils) rich in leafmould. Spreading clones like 'Springwood White' and 'Springwood Pink' are most effective. Several other *Erica* species and hybrids are equally as effective for acid soils including *E. vagans* and E. × *darleyensis*. (see p.35).
Euonymus fortunei var. *radicans*	B Carpeter e	Medium	High	9 (23)	12–18 (30–46)	High	Dense evergreen for sun or shade. 'Kewensis' is a small-leaved variant 3–4 inches (7–10 cm) high which should be planted 9 inches (23 cm) apart to form dense ground cover. Occasional trimming required.
Euonymus fortunei f. *carrierei*	B Hummock e	Medium	High	24 (60)	30 (75)	Medium	The 'adult' shrubby form of var.*radicans*. Several forms with variegated leaves are effective for ground cover. 'Emerald 'n Gold', 'Emerald Gaiety' and 'Coloratus' are all good.
Euphorbia robbiae	D Coloniser (Suckers) e	Medium	High	15 (38)	18 (46)	High	Sometimes slow to establish but then spreads freely. Greenish flowers.

Deciduous = d Evergreen = e Semi-evergreen = s-e

Name	*Group & Habit*	*Speed of Growth*	*Density of Cover*	*Approx. Height inches (cm)*	*Average Planting Distance inches (cm)*	*Shade Tolerance*	*Special Remarks*
Galeobdolon argentatum (*Lamium galeobdolon* 'Variegatum')	A Coloniser (Carpeter) e	Rapid	High	6–9 (15–23)	24–36 (60–90)	High	Marbled foliage and yellow flowers. Tremendous vigour. Excellent under trees or shrubs – not for areas with small plants which will be smothered.
×*Gaulnettya* 'Wisley Pearl'	B Coloniser (Suckers) e	Medium	Medium-high	24–36 (60–90)	24 (60)	High	Hybrid of *Gaultheria shallon* and *Pernettya mucronata*. Fairly dense cover. Flowers white, fruit purplish red. Acid 'leafy' soil.
Gaultheria procumbens (see p.43)	D Coloniser (Suckers) e	Medium	Medium	6 (15)	12–15 (30–38)	High	Acid soils. Will tolerate dry conditions once established.
Genista hispanica (see p.42)	B Hummock d	Medium	High	24 (60)	24 (60)	Low	Sun and good drainage. Dense spring growth.
Genista lydia	B Hummock d	Medium	Medium	12–15 (30–38)	18–21 (46–54)	Low	Sun and good drainage.

Name	*Group & Habit*	*Speed of Growth*	*Density of Cover*	*Approx. Height inches (cm)*	*Average Planting Distance inches (cm)*	*Shade Tolerance*	*Special Remarks*
Genista pilosa	B Carpeter d	Medium	High	12 (30)	15–18 (38–46)	Low	Sun or light shade. Good drainage. useful on banks. 'Procumbens' is a prostrate clone.
Genista (Chamaespartium) sagittalis	B Hummock or Carpeter d	Medium	Medium-high	9–12 (23–30)	12–15 (30–38)	Low	Winged stems. Dense cover once established. Sun and good drainage. *G. delphinensis* is similar but smaller.
Geranium endressii (see p.43)	C Clump d	Medium	High	12–21 (30–54)	12–15 (30–38)	Medium	Dense cover and continuous pink flowers in summer. 'Wargrave Pink' is the clone commonly available. 'Claridge Druce' (*endressii* × *versicolor*) is more vigorous and forms equally dense cover. Both spread widely from the central rosette of buds and the old foliage remains as a cover all winter.
Geranium himalayense	D Coloniser (Suckers) d	Medium	High	9–12 (23–30)	12–15 (30–38)	Medium	Tolerant of shade but best in open positions. Violet-blue flowers. 'Johnson's Blue' is a hybrid of this species and *G. pratense* with paler blue flowers.

Deciduous = d   Evergreen = e   Semi-evergreen = s-e

Name	*Group & Habit*	*Speed of Growth*	*Density of Cover*	*Approx. Height inches (cm)*	*Average Planting Distance inches (cm)*	*Shade Tolerance*	*Special Remarks*
Geranium macrorrhizum	D Coloniser (Carpeter) d	Medium	Medium-high	9–12 (23–30)	12–15 (30–38)	Medium	Flowers magenta to pink or white. Extremely dense cover, and scented foliage.
Geranium × *magnificum*	D Clump d	Medium	High	9–12 (23–30)	12–15 (30–38)	Medium	Withstands hot sun. Violet-blue flowers. Dense summer cover. *G. ibericum* and *G. platypetalum* are similar.
Geranium phaeum	D Clump d	Medium	Medium-high	12 (30)	15–18 (38–46)	High	Excellent in shade. Maroon to white flowers. *G. punctatum* is a close relative also good in shade. *G. nodosum* (flowers lilac) is very tolerant of deep shade.
Geranium procurrens	D Coloniser (Carpeter) d	Rapid	High	9–12 (23–30)	18–24 (46–60)	Medium	Widespreading growths rooting down to limited extent. Mauve flowers.
Geranium psilostemon	C Clump d	Medium	High	30 (75)	24–36 (60–90)	Medium-low	Bright magenta flowers. Good summer cover.

Name	*Group & Habit*	*Speed of Growth*	*Density of Cover*	*Approx. Height inches (cm)*	*Average Planting Distance inches (cm)*	*Shade Tolerance*	*Special Remarks*
Geranium 'Russell Prichard'	D Coloniser (Carpeter) d	Rapid	High	6–9 (15–23)	12–15 (30–38)	Low	Requires full sun and good drainage. Grey foliage and pink flowers. Dense trails of foliage in summer which do not root down but die back in winter. May be slightly tender in cold areas. *G. wallichianum* has a similar growth habit but violet-purple flowers. It is quite hardy.
Geranium sanguineum (see p.42)	D Coloniser (Suckers) d	Medium	Medium-high	6–9 (15–23)	12–15 (30–38)	Medium-low	Magenta to white flowers. Best in open or slightly shaded positions; ssp. *lancastriense* is semi-prostrate with pink veined flowers.
Geranium sylvaticum	C Clump e	Medium	High	12–15 (30–38)	15–18 (38–46)	High	Sun to fairly deep shade. Lavender-blue to white flowers. Seeds freely.
Gerum × borisii	C Clump d	Medium	Medium	6–9 (15–23)	12 (30)	Medium	Bright orange flowers.

Deciduous = d   Evergreen = e   Semi-evergreen = s-e

Above, left: *Geranium sanguineum* ssp. *lancastriense*, a semi-prostrate form, best in open or slightly shaded position. (see page 41)
Above, right: *Dryas octopetala*, a carpeter which produces fluffy seed heads. (see page 36)
Below, left: *Genista hispanica*, the Spanish gorse, a shrub which thrives in full sun. (see page 38)
Below, right: *Dicentra formosa*, a suckering plant which prefers shade and a moist soil. (see page 36)

Top: *Gaultheria procumbens*, a dwarf shrub for acid soils. (see page 38)
Below: *Geranium endressii*, a herbaceous plant providing dense cover and freely produced pink flowers throughout the summer. (see page 39)

Name	*Group & Habit*	*Speed of Growth*	*Density of Cover*	*Approx. Height inches (cm)*	*Average Planting Distance inches (cm)*	*Shade Tolerance*	*Special Remarks*
Glechoma (*Nepeta*) *hederacea* 'Variegata' (Variegated ground ivy)	D Coloniser (Carpeter) e	Medium-rapid	Medium	3–4 (8–10)	18–24 (46–60)	Medium	The green-leaved form is a rampageous weed. The variegated form is less rapid in growth and some weeding is needed in the first year or two.
× *Halimiocistus sahucii*	B Hummock e	Medium	Medium-high	12 (30)	21–24 (54–60)	Low	Full sun and good drainage. Hardy in all but the coldest gardens in Britain. Profusion of white flowers in summer.
Halimium lasianthum	B Hummock e	Medium	Medium	12 (30)	18–24 (46–60)	Low	Full sun, good drainage. Damaged in severe winters. Flowers yellow or yellow with crimson base.
Hebe albicans	B Hummock e	Medium	High	12 (30)	18–24 (46–60)	Low	Full sun. Grey foliage, dense cover. 'Pewter Dome' is a fine clone with narrower leaves.
Hebe chathamica	D Coloniser (Carpeter) e	Medium-rapid	Medium-high	4–6 (10–15)	18–24 (46–60)	Low	Branches spread rapidly and root down. Less dense and patchy in shade. Green foliage.

Name	*Group & Habit*	*Speed of Growth*	*Density of Cover*	*Approx. Height inches (cm)*	*Average Planting Distance inches (cm)*	*Shade Tolerance*	*Special Remarks*
Hebe 'Pagei'	B Hummock or Coloniser (Carpeter) e	Medium	Medium	6–9 (15–23)	15 (38)	Low	Sometimes rooting down as it spreads. May die out in centre and requires trimming in April to encourage re-growth.
Hebe rakaiensis	B Hummock e	Medium	High	18–24 (46–60)	21–24 (54–60)	Low	Dense light green mounds of foliage. Full sun. *H. vernicosa* is of similar habit but with darker foliage.
Hedera canariensis 'Azorica'	A Coloniser (Carpeter) e	Rapid	High	6–9 (15–23)	36–48 (90–120)	High	Dense shade to full sun. Dark green leaves, 'Gloire de Marengo' ('Variegata') with leaves marked white, grey and green is unreliable in cold gardens.
Hedera colchica	A Coloniser (Carpeter) e	Rapid	High	6–9 (15–23)	36–48 (90–120)	High	Dark green foliage. Dense shade to full sun. The following are equally effective: 'Dentata' has paler, larger leaves. 'Dentata Variegata' has a creamy-yellow margin and appears as hardy as the type. 'Sulphur Heart' has gold-centred foliage.

Deciduous = d   Evergreen = e   Semi-evergreen = s-e

Name	*Group & Habit*	*Speed of Growth*	*Density of Cover*	*Approx. Height inches (cm)*	*Average Planting Distance inches (cm)*	*Shade Tolerance*	*Special Remarks*
Hedera helix (Common ivy)	A Coloniser (Carpeter) e	Rapid	High	6–12 (15–30)	24–48 (depending on vigour) (60–120)	High	Extremely variable; many clones make first class ground cover. Var. *hibernica*, the Irish Ivy, is of dense and very vigorous growth and rapidly covers the ground. Other smaller cultivars include 'Green Ripple', 'Pittsburgh', 'Gold-heart', and 'Très Coupé'. Many others – with variegated or green leaves – are suitable.
Helianthemum hybrids	B Hummock e	Medium	High	6–9 (15–23)	12–18 (30–46)	Low	Full sun and good drainage. Straggly in shade. Ideal for sunny banks. Many colours and single or double flowers. 'Wisley Pink' and 'Wisley Primrose' are dense grey-leaved clones. Cut back after flowering.
Helianthemum nummularium 'Amy Baring'	B Hummock e	Medium	High	4–6 (10–15)	12–18 (30–46)	Low	Grey leaves and orange-yellow flowers. Dense spreading growth. Full sun. Cut back after flowering.
Hemerocallis fulva (Day-lily)	C Clump or Coloniser (Suckers) d	Medium	Medium	18–24 (46–60)	18 (46)	Medium	Arching foliage forming dense summer cover. Sun or some shade. Most species (*H. minor* and other dwarfs excepted) and the hybrids are reasonably effective.

Name	*Group & Habit*	*Speed of Growth*	*Density of Cover*	*Approx. Height inches (cm)*	*Average Planting Distance inches (cm)*	*Shade Tolerance*	*Special Remarks*
Hosta crispula	C Clump d	Medium	Medium-high	12 (30)	15–18 (38–46)	High	Long pointed spreading foliage, margined white.
Hosta decorata	C Clump d	Medium	Medium-high	9–12 (23–30)	15 (38)	High	Blunt, broad leaves, white margin. As with most hostas, the thick 'rootstocks' are more easily divided after five years, rather than ten.
Hosta elata (*H. montana*)	C Clump d	Medium	Medium-high	18 (46)	18 (46)	High	Large mid-green foliage, forming very dense summer cover.
Hosta fortunei	C Clump d	Medium	Medium-high	18 (46)	18 (46)	High	Many variants make good summer cover. 'Obscura Marginata' and 'Albopicta', are two fine variegated clones; 'Obscura', 'Hyacinthina' and f. *rugosa* are the best of the green leaved forms.
Hosta plantaginea	C Clump d	Medium	Medium-high	15 (38)	15 (38)	High	Pale green arching foliage, scented white flowers in late summer. Flowers best in moist soil and warm position.

Deciduous = d   Evergreen = e   Semi-evergreen = s-e

Name	*Group & Habit*	*Speed of Growth*	*Density of Cover*	*Approx. Height inches (cm)*	*Average Planting Distance inches (cm)*	*Shade Tolerance*	*Special Remarks*
Hosta rectifolia	C Clump d	Medium	Medium-high	18 (46)	18 (46)	High	Long, relatively narrow foliage; 'Tall Boy' is a very vigorous relation, and makes excellent cover with attractive lilac flowers in summer.
Hosta sieboldiana	C Clump d	Medium	Medium-high	18 (46)	18–24 (46–60)	High	Huge leaves, blue-grey (var. *elegans*) or grey-green. The variegated 'Frances Williams' is almost as vigorous.
Hosta undulata erromena	C Clump d	Medium	Medium-high	18 (46)	18 (46)	High	Glossy green, long leaves and tall spikes of purple flowers. The variegated *H. undulata* var. *undulata* and var. *univittata* are smaller foliaged and less dense.
Hosta ventricosa (see p. 13)	C Clump d	Medium	Medium-high	15 (38)	18 (46)	High	Dark shining green foliage and fine violet-purple flowers. Two variegated clones 'Variegata' and 'Aureomaculata' are good but slightly less vigorous.
Hypericum calycinum (St John's wort)	A Coloniser (Sucker) e	Rapid	High	9–12 (23–30)	15–18 (38–46)	High	Sun or shade, any well drained soil. Cut to near ground level each April to obtain densest cover. (see p.11)

Name	*Group & Habit*	*Speed of Growth*	*Density of Cover*	*Approx. Height inches (cm)*	*Average Planting Distance inches (cm)*	*Shade Tolerance*	*Special Remarks*
Hypericum cerastioides (H. rhodopeum)	B Coloniser (Carpeter) e	Medium	Medium	3 (8)	9–12 (23–30)	Low	Greyish foliage. Full sun, well-drained soil. May die out in shade.
Hypericum × moserianum	B Hummock or Coloniser (Suckers) e	Medium	Medium	18 (46)	18–21 (46–54)	Medium	Good low cover but can be damaged in severe winters. Best in sunny, well drained position.
Iberis sempervirens	B Hummock e	Medium	Medium-high	9–12 (23–30)	12–15 (30–38)	Low	Sunny, well drained position. Dark green leaves and white flowers. 'Snowflake' is a compact dense clone.
Iris foetidissima	C Clump (rhizomes) e	Medium	Medium	18 (46)	12–15 (30–38)	High	Deep shade and often dry soil but thrives in any soil and site unless poorly drained. Dark green arching foliage. 'Citrina' fruits well.

Deciduous = d　Evergreen = e　Semi-evergreen = s-e

Name	*Group & Habit*	*Speed of Growth*	*Density of Cover*	*Approx. Height inches (cm)*	*Average Planting Distance inches (cm)*	*Shade Tolerance*	*Special Remarks*
Juniperus communis var. *jackii*	B Hummock or Carpeter e	Medium	Medium-high	6–9 (15–23)	24 (60)	Low	Occasionally rooting down. Low spreading habit. Several other variants are equally useful, – ssp. *depressa*, 'Depressa Aurea', 'Dumosa', 'Effusa' and 'Repanda' amongst them.
Juniperus conferta	B Hummock or Carpeter e	Medium	High	6–9 (15–23)	24 (60)	Medium	May root down. Tolerates some shade.
Juniperus horizontalis	B Hummock or Carpeter e	Medium	Medium	6 (15)	18–24 (46–60)	Low	Several clones with glaucous, bronze or green foliage are available. Forms dense mats eventually but weeding needed in early years.
Juniperus × *media* 'Pfitzeriana'	B Hummock e	Medium	High	36 (90)	48–72 (120–180)	High	Will withstand dense shade of trees. High ground cover. The golden-foliaged variants are less vigorous.
Juniperus sabina var. *tamariscifolia*	B Hummock e	Medium-slow	High	15–18 (38–46)	24–30 (60–75)	Medium	Dense cover but relatively slow. Withstands some shade.

Name	*Group & Habit*	*Speed of Growth*	*Density of Cover*	*Approx. Height inches (cm)*	*Average Planting Distance inches (cm)*	*Shade Tolerance*	*Special Remarks*
Lamium maculatum	D Coloniser (Carpeter) e	Rapid	Medium-high	3–4 (8–10)	12–15 (30–38)	High	Variegated leaves and magenta, pink or white flowers. May die out in patches occasionally but usually excellent ground cover.
Leucothoe fontanesiana	B Coloniser (Carpeter) e	Medium	High	36 (90)	30–36 (75–90)	High	Shade and leafy, acid soil.
Liriope muscari	C Clump e	Medium-slow	Medium-high	9 (23)	9–12 (23–30)	Medium-low	Sunny dry position. Thinner growth in shade. (see p.21)
Lithodora (Lithospermum) diffusa	B Hummock e	Medium	Medium	9 (23)	12–15 (30–38)	Medium-low	Sunny open position in acid soils. Will grow in partial shade but often thinner in growth. 'Grace Ward' and 'Heavenly Blue' are two clones offered. Tends to die out in patches.

Deciduous = d Evergreen = e Semi-evergreen = s-e

Name	*Group & Habit*	*Speed of Growth*	*Density of Cover*	*Approx. Height inches (cm)*	*Average Planting Distance inches (cm)*	*Shade Tolerance*	*Special Remarks*
Lonicera pileata	B Hummock e	Medium	High	18 (46)	24–30 (60–75)	High	Roots down occasionally. Any well drained soil in sun/shade. *L. nitida* 'Graziosa' is similar, a dense spreading shrub with neat, small dark foliage.
Luzula maxima (*L. sylvatica*) (Woodrush)	D Coloniser (Suckers) e	Medium	Medium-high	12 (30)	12–15 (30–38)	High	Good for shady areas, often in dry situations. Spreads quickly forming solid mats of grassy foliage. 'Variegata' is a clone with white edged leaves. Useful in difficult places.
Lysimachia nummularia (Creeping Jenny)	D Coloniser (Carpeter) e	Medium	Medium-high	1–2 (2–5)	12–15 (30–38)	Medium	Dense carpets for moist sites in sun or shade. Yellow flowers. 'Aurea', the gold-leafed form is very attractive but less vigorous and may be scorched in sun. Some weeding in first year.
Mahonia aquifolium	B Coloniser (Suckers) e	Medium-slow	Medium-high	24 (36) (60 (90))	24 (60)	High	Cut back in April each year to encourage dense habit. Will grow well in shade and dry soil if mulched annually. *M. repens rotundifolia* is taller but equally as dense when mature. Both are sometimes slow to become established.

Name	*Group & Habit*	*Speed of Growth*	*Density of Cover*	*Approx. Height inches (cm)*	*Average Planting Distance inches (cm)*	*Shade Tolerance*	*Special Remarks*
Maianthemum bifolium	D Coloniser (Suckers) d	Medium	Medium	4–5 (10–13)	12–15 (30–38)	High	Cool leaf-mould soil in shade. Does not always make a dense carpet.
Muehlenbeckia axillaris	D Coloniser (Suckers) d	Medium-high	Medium-high	6–9 (15–23)	18 (46)	Medium	Best in full sun when an intricate network of branches develops into a solid mass. Can smother small plants.
Nepeta × *faassenii*	C Clump e	Medium	Medium	9 (23)	12 (30)	Low	Best in full sun, good drainage. Cut back old growth in spring. Tends to die out if cut back in autumn.
Omphalodes cappadocica	D Coloniser (Carpeter) d	Medium	Medium	6 (15)	12 (30)	High	Best in shade, will tolerate sun in moist conditions. Very good for humus-rich soils. Blue flowers. *O. verna* (Blue eyed Mary) is smaller but good in shade.
Origanum vulgare 'Aureum' (Marjoram)	C Clump d	Medium	Medium	6 (15)	12 (30)	Low	Winter rosettes of golden foliage which develop to good summer cover in open, well-drained sites. Poor in shade. *O. vulgare* is as good but less ornamental.

Deciduous = d Evergreen = e Semi-evergreen = s-e

Name	*Group & Habit*	*Speed of Growth*	*Density of Cover*	*Approx. Height inches (cm)*	*Average Planting Distance inches (cm)*	*Shade Tolerance*	*Special Remarks*
Osteospermum jucundum (Dimorphotheca barberiae)	B Hummock e	Medium	Medium-high	6–9 (15–23)	15–18 (38–46)	Low	Mat-forming, particularly 'Compactum'. Sunny well-drained site. Not fully hardy in cold, wet areas. 'Nairobi Purple' with deep purple flowers is less hardy, but excellent summer cover.
Oxalis oregana	D Coloniser (Suckers) d	Medium	Medium	6 (15)	9–12 (23–30)	High	Fairly dense summer cover in leafy woodland soil. Rich green, clover-like leaves, flowers white to purplish pink. Scaly rootstock and *not* increasing by bulbils.
Pachyphragma macrophyllum	C Clump d	Medium	Medium	6–9 (15–23)	12–15 (30–38)	High	Good summer cover from the rounded glossy leaves. Attractive white flowers in May. Shade and reasonably moist soil.
Pachysandra terminalis	B Carpeter e	Medium	High	3–4 (8–10)	9–12 (23–30)	High	Excellent cover in dry shade; acid or alkaline soils. 'Variegata' is marginally less vigorous.
Parahebe catarractae	B Hummock d	Medium	Medium	9 (23)	12 (30)	Low	Open sunny position in well-drained soil. Flowers white or blue-purple. *P. lyallii* is similar but has smaller foliage, of more prostrate habit, the branches often rooting down.

Name	*Group & Habit*	*Speed of Growth*	*Density of Cover*	*Approx. Height inches (cm)*	*Average Planting Distance inches (cm)*	*Shade Tolerance*	*Special Remarks*
Pernettya mucronata	B Coloniser (Suckers) e	Medium	Medium-high	24–36 (60–90)	24 (60)	Medium-low	Full sun and an acid soil. In shade less dense. (see p.10)
Pernettya prostrata spp. *pentlandii*	B Coloniser (Suckers) e	Medium	High	12–18 (30–46)	15 (38)	Medium	Sun and an acid soil. Usually of dense spreading growth.
Phlomis fruticosa (Jerusalem sage)	B Hummock e	Medium	High	36 (90)	30–36 (75–90)	Low	Dense high cover for an open sunny site. Best in warm gardens. Flowers yellow and grey-green leaves. *P. chrysophylla* is similar but lower in habit with golden-green foliage. Both are excellent for dry sunny banks.
Phlox subulata and *P. douglasii*	D Coloniser (Carpeter) d	Medium	High	3–4 (8–10)	9–12 (23–30)	Medium-low	Best in full sun and good drainage. Less dense and tends to become patchy in shade. Numerous hybrids 'Temiscaming', 'May Snow', 'Chattahoochee' and many others can be useful.

Deciduous = d   Evergreen = e   Semi-evergreen = s-e

Name	*Group & Habit*	*Speed of Growth*	*Density of Cover*	*Approx. Height inches (cm)*	*Average Planting Distance inches (cm)*	*Shade Tolerance*	*Special Remarks*
Polygonum affine	D Coloniser (Carpeter) d	Medium	Medium-high	2–3 (5–8)	9–12 (23–30)	Low	'Darjeeling Red' and 'Superbum' (deep pink) are reliable. 'Donald Lowndes' tends to die out in patches and is sometimes disappointing ground cover. Sun or light shade.
Polygonum campanulatum	C Clump d	Medium-rapid	High	18–24 (46–60)	18–24 (46–60)	Medium	Winter rosettes develop wide-spreading dense trails of foliage. *Not* invasive. Long lasting pink or white flowers all summer. Good in moist or wet soils.
Polygonum vacciniifolium	D Coloniser (Carpeter) d	Medium	High	3–4 (8–10)	9–12 (23–30)	Low	Open sunny position. Sometimes slow to become established but dense cover later. Valuable for pink flowers in September-October.
Potentilla alba	D Coloniser (Carpeter) d	Medium	Medium	2–3 (5–8)	9–12 (23–30)	Medium	Sun or some shade, leaves green above, grey below. Flowers white. Dense when established.

Name	Group & Habit	Speed of Growth	Density of Cover	Approx. Height inches (cm)	Average Planting Distance inches (cm)	Shade Tolerance	Special Remarks
Potentilla calabra	D Coloniser (Carpeter) s-e	Medium	Medium	2–3 (5–8)	9–12 (23–30)	Low	Open, sunny, well-drained site. May die back in patches during the winter. Greyish white foliage, flowers yellow. *P. argentea* is similar but with green upper leaf surfaces.
Potentilla fruticosa var. *mandschurica*	B Hummock d	Medium	Medium-high	15–18 (38–46)	24–30 (60–75)	Low	Open sunny position, any reasonably drained soil. Straggly in shade. Several clones of *P. fruticosa* and related species are of spreading dense habit including 'Long-acre', 'Elizabeth' and *farreri*.
Prunella grandiflora	D Coloniser (Carpeter) e	Medium	Medium	3–4 (8–10)	12 (30)	Medium	Sun or some shade. Not on dry sandy soils. 'Loveliness' has pink flowers and a white clone is also grown.
Prunus laurocerasus 'Otto Luyken'	B Hummock e	Medium	High	36 (90)	36–48 (90–120)	High	Excellent high cover, sun or shade, any but poorly drained soils. 'Zabeliana' and 'Schip-kaensis' are both spreading in habit and equally good for ground cover.

Deciduous = d Evergreen = e Semi-evergreen = s-e

Name	*Group & Habit*	*Speed of Growth*	*Density of Cover*	*Approx. Height inches (cm)*	*Average Planting Distance inches (cm)*	*Shade Tolerance*	*Special Remarks*
Pulmonaria species and hybrids (Lungworts) (see p.11)	C Clump d or e	Medium	Medium-high	5–6 (13–15)	12 (30)	High	Sun or shade. Almost all are effective easy ground covers. *P. angustifolia* (flowers blue) dies back to central rosettes in winter. 'Mawson's Variety' and 'Azurea' are good clones. *P. officinalis* and *P. saccharata* (*P. picta*) have foliage spotted white to varying degrees and retain much of the foliage during winter. *P. rubra* has pale, almost evergreen leaves and red flowers.
Rhododendrons	Many are effective as ground cover in acid woodland conditions. None is listed here as individual preference for flower colour and habit will dictate the choice.						
Roses	A few are sometimes recommended including 'Max Graf', *R.* × *paulii*, 'Temple Bells', 'Nozomi', and *R. wichuraiana*. They all require weeding for two seasons after planting and sometimes more. At Wisley 'Temple Bells' has proved the most effective, fully covering the ground in two seasons, planted at 36–48 in (90–120 cm) apart.						
Rosmarinus lavandulaceus (Rosemary)	B Hummock e	Medium	High	4 (10)	24–36 (60–90)	Low	Prostrate growth, not fully hardy but ideal for sunny dry banks except in cold gardens. Also known as *R. officinalis prostratus*.
Rubus calycinoides (*R. fockeanus*)	D Coloniser (Carpeter) e	Medium	Medium-high	2–3 (5–8)	12–15 (30–38)	High	Sun or shade, all but poorly drained soils, dense cover.

Name	*Group & Habit*	*Speed of Growth*	*Density of Cover*	*Approx. Height inches (cm)*	*Average Planting Distance inches (cm)*	*Shade Tolerance*	*Special Remarks*
Rubus tricolor	D Coloniser (Carpeter) e	Rapid	Medium	12 (30)	36–48 (90–120)	High	Strong growing but weeding needed during first year or two. Sun or shade, all but poorly drained soils.
Salvia officinalis (Common sage)	B Hummock e	Medium	High	12–18 (30–46)	18–24 (46–60)	Low	Full sun, well drained soil. Poor in wet conditions. 'Purpurascens' (foliage purplish) and 'Icterina' (yellow variegated leaves) are slightly less vigorous and may become thin after a few seasons.
Sarcococca humilis	D Coloniser (Suckers) e	Medium	Medium-high	9–15 (23–38)	12–15 (30–38)	High	Shady positions in leaf-enriched soil but will grow well in sandy dry places if not in hot sun. *S. confusa*, *S. ruscifolia* and other species are also useful but less wide spreading.
Saxifraga 'mossy' hybrids	D Coloniser (Carpeter) e	Medium	Modium-high	2–3 (5–8)	12 (30)	Low	Good cover in sunny positions in all but poorly drained soils. May die out in patches.

Deciduous = d   Evergreen = e   Semi-evergreen = s-e

Name	*Group & Habit*	*Speed of Growth*	*Density of Cover*	*Approx. Height inches (cm)*	*Average Planting Distance inches (cm)*	*Shade Tolerance*	*Special Remarks*
Sedum spathulifolium	D Coloniser (Carpeter) e	Medium	Medium	2–3 (5–8)	9–12 (23–30)	Low	Purplish or greyish-white leaves. Sun and reasonable drainage.
Sedum spurium	D Coloniser (Carpeter) e	Medium	Medium	2–3 (5–8)	9–12 (23–30)	Low	Sun and reasonable drainage. 'Green Mantle' is a non-flowering clone, forming dense carpets.
Senecio 'Sunshine' (*S. laxifolius* and *S. greyi* of gardens)	B Hummock e	Medium	High	36 (90)	36–48 (90–120)	Low	Sun and good drainage. Grey foliage, yellow flowers. Dense high cover.
Skimmia japonica 'Bowles' Dwarf'	B Hummock and Coloniser (Carpeter) e	Medium	High	12 (30)	18 (46)	High	Shade in all but poorly drained soils. Low dense cover, seldom flowers. Other clones produce higher cover including 'Rubella', 'Fragrans' and 'Foremanii'.

Name	*Group & Habit*	*Speed of Growth*	*Density of Cover*	*Approx. Height inches (cm)*	*Average Planting Distance inches (cm)*	*Shade Tolerance*	*Special Remarks*
Stachys byzantina 'Silver Carpet' (Lamb's ears)	D Coloniser (Carpeter) e	Medium	High	3–4 (8–10)	12–15 (30–38)	Low	Sun, well drained soil. Carpets of silver foliage. Poor and scraggy in shade. Non- or sparse-flowering clone. Also known as S. *lanata* 'Silver Carpet'.
Stephanandra incisa 'Crispa'	D Coloniser (Carpeter) d	Medium	Medium	18–24 (46–60)	36 (90)	Low	Sun and open position. Forms a low network of arching branches with pretty, cut leaves.
Symphoricarpos × *chenaultii* 'Hancock'	D Coloniser (Suckers & Carpeter) d	Medium	Medium	18–24 (46–60)	36 (90)	Medium-low	Thinner in shade. Suckering habit, forming mounds of arching branches.
Symphytum grandiflorum	D Coloniser (Suckers & Carpeters) d	Medium-rapid	High	6 (15)	12 (30)	High	Excellent in shade, covering ground rapidly. Moist but not wet soils are best but grows well even in relatively dry soils. Yellow, pink or blue flowers in spring.

Deciduous = d Evergreen = e Semi-evergreen = s-e

Name	*Group & Habit*	*Speed of Growth*	*Density of Cover*	*Approx. Height inches (cm)*	*Average Planting Distance inches (cm)*	*Shade Tolerance*	*Special Remarks*
Tellima grandiflora 'Purpurea'	D Coloniser (Carpeter) e	Medium	High	6 (15)	12 (30)	High	Purple foliage in winter. Shade and sun, any soil unless poorly drained. Pinkish flowers.
Thymus serpyllum (Thyme)	D Coloniser (Carpeter) e	Medium	High	1 (2)	9 (23)	Low	Full sun, good drainage. Several vigorous clones with lilac, pink or white flowers including 'Pink Chintz' are good.
Tiarella cordifolia	D Coloniser (Carpeter) e	Medium	High	3–4 (8–10)	12–15 (30–38)	High	Leaf-enriched soil in shade, occasionally does well in sun. Excellent cover. Green bronze-tinted leaves. *T. wherryi* is also good but slower.
Vaccinium vitis-idaea	D Coloniser (Carpeter) e	Medium	Medium	6 (15)	9–12 (23–30)	High	Acid soil, humus and shade. Bronze-tinted leaves in winter; pinkish bell-like flowers in summer.
Vancouveria hexandra	D Coloniser (Suckers) d	Medium	Medium	6 (15)	12 (30)	High	Shade and humus – rich soil for best results. Will tolerate open positions but is less vigorous. Divided foliage, white sprays of flowers in spring.

Name	*Group & Habit*	*Speed of Growth*	*Density of Cover*	*Approx. Height inches (cm)*	*Average Planting Distance inches (cm)*	*Shade Tolerance*	*Special Remarks*
Veronica prostrata	D Coloniser (Carpeter) e	Medium	Medium	1–2 (2–5)	9–12 (23–30)	Low	Sun and well-drained soil. Flowers blue. Several clones including 'Kapitan' and 'Spode Blue' are suitable.
Vinca major (Larger periwinkle)	A Coloniser (Carpeter) e	Rapid	High	6–9 (15–23)	18 (46)	High	Flowers blue or white. Ideal cover for almost any situation except poorly drained soils. Acid or alkaline soils from deep shade to open conditions. Less dense on very dry exposed sites. Initial weeding required. 'Elegantissima' with variegated foliage is equally good. Cut back hard after flowering.
Vinca major ssp. *hirsuta*	A Coloniser (Carpeter) e	Rapid	High	6–9 (15–23)	18–24 (46–60)	High	Very vigorous, eventually forming dense rampant cover. Starry flowers.
Vinca minor (Lesser periwinkle)	A Coloniser (Carpeter) e	Rapid	High	4–6 (10–15)	15–18 (38–46)	High	Smaller foliage but very effective in similar conditions. Several named clones with variegated foliage and single or double flowers in white, blue or purple are available. All are useful.

Deciduous = d   Evergreen = e   Semi-evergreen = s-e

Name	*Group & Habit*	*Speed of Growth*	*Density of Cover*	*Approx. Height inches (cm)*	*Average Planting Distance inches (cm)*	*Shade Tolerance*	*Special Remarks*
Viola cornuta	D Coloniser (Carpeter) e	Medium	High	3–4 (8–10)	9–12 (23–30)	Medium	Cool, open position, good drainage. Straggly on dry soils. White or lilac-purple flowers.
Viola 'Huntercombe Purple' (see p.6)	D Coloniser (Carpeter) e	Medium	High	3–4 (8–10)	9–12 (23–30)	Medium	Deep purple flowers. Several clones equally effective including 'Haslemere' (lavender-pink), 'Connie' (white) and 'Martin' (deep purple). Same conditions as *V. cornuta*.
Viola labradorica (of gardens).	D Coloniser (Suckers) s-e	Medium	Medium	2–3 (5–8)	9–12 (23–30)	High	Good in dense shade or sun. Runs freely underground and can become a nuisance. Foliage purple-flushed.
Viola obliqua (*V. cucullata*)	D Coloniser (Suckers) d	Medium-slow	Medium	3–4 (8–10)	12 (30)	High	Dense summer cover from foliage slowly forming compact mats. Easy in any but boggy soils. White or purple flowers.
Waldsteinia ternata	A Coloniser (Carpeter) e	High	High	3–4 (8–10)	12 (30)	High	Dry or moist soils in full sun to deep shade. Excellent cover, mats of thick evergreen leaves and yellow flowers.

Deciduous = d   Evergreen = e   Semi-evergreen = s-e